WRITE YOUR OWN

AUTOBIOGRAPHY

by Natalie M. Rosinsky

Compass Point Books ✤ Minneapolis, Minnesota

Compass Point Books
151 Good Counsel Drive
P.O. Box 669
Mankato, MN 56002-0669

 This book was manufactured with paper containing
at least 10 percent post-consumer waste.

Managing Editor: Catherine Neitge
Page Production: Bobbie Nuytten
Photo Researcher: Svetlana Zhurkin
Library Consultant: Kathleen Baxter

Creative Director: Keith Griffin
Editorial Director: Nick Healy

Compass Point Books would like to acknowledge the contributions of Tish Farrell, who
authored earlier Write Your Own books and whose supporting text is reused in part herein.

Library of Congress Cataloging-in-Publication Data
Rosinsky, Natalie M. (Natalie Myra)
  Write your own autobiography / by Natalie M. Rosinsky.
    p. cm.
  Includes index.
  ISBN 978-0-7565-3525-4 (library binding)
  ISBN 978-0-7565-3526-1 (paperback)
  1. Autobiography—Authorship. I. Title.
  CT25.R675 2008
  808'.06692—dc22   2007033092

Visit Compass Point Books on the Internet at *www.compasspointbooks.com*
or e-mail your request to *custserv@compasspointbooks.com*

About the Author
Natalie M. Rosinsky is the award-winning author of
more than 100 works for young readers. She earned
graduate degrees from the University of Wisconsin-
Madison and has been a high school teacher and
college professor as well as a corporate trainer. Natalie,
who reads and writes in Mankato, Minnesota, says,
"My love of reading led me to write. I take pleasure in
framing ideas, crafting words, detailing other lives and
places. I am delighted to share these joys with young

See Inside Yourself

Take an eye-opening look at yourself—inside and out! Knowing yourself is important as you write your own autobiography. An autobiography is much more than a list of facts. Which people, places, and events have shaped your life? How would you describe yourself today? What kind of person do you hope to be tomorrow? What are your plans and dreams for your life five years—or even 25 years—from now?

As you write your own autobiography, you will discover answers to these questions. This information may even change your life! This book will help you start and complete this adventure of a lifetime. It contains brainstorming and training activities to sharpen your writing skills. Tips and advice from famous writers and examples from their own work will also help you to explore and explain what you see inside yourself.

CONTENTS

WANT TO BE A WRITER?

This book is the perfect place to start. It aims to give you the tools to write your own autobiography. Learn how to craft believable portraits of people and how to plot your own life story with a satisfying beginning, middle, and ending. Examples from famous books appear throughout, with tips and techniques from published authors to help you on your way.

Get the writing habit

Do timed and regular practice. Real writers learn to write even when they don't particularly feel like it.

Create an autobiography-writing zone.

Keep a journal.

Carry a notebook—record interesting events and note how people behave and speak.

Generate ideas

Figure out what you hope to achieve by writing your autobiography. What do you want to learn about yourself? What are your problems and accomplishments?

Brainstorm to find out everything about your family and other important people in your life.

Research settings, events, creatures, and items in your life.

Create a timeline of your life.

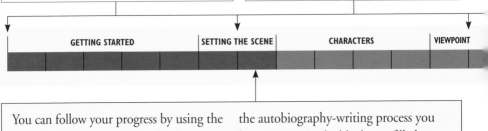

| GETTING STARTED | SETTING THE SCENE | CHARACTERS | VIEWPOINT |

You can follow your progress by using the bar located on the bottom of each page. The orange color tells you how far along the autobiography-writing process you have gotten. As the blocks are filled out, your autobiography will be growing.

Plan

What parts of your life is your autobiography about?

What happens?

Plan beginning, middle, and end.

Write a synopsis or create storyboards.

Write

Write the first draft, then put it aside for a while.

Check spelling and dialogue—does it flow?

Remove unnecessary words.

Does the autobiography have a good title and satisfying ending?

Avoid clichés.

Publish

Write or print the final draft.

Always keep a copy for yourself.

Send your autobiography to children's magazines, Internet writing sites, competitions, or school magazines.

SYNOPSES AND PLOTS | WINNING WORDS | SCINTILLATING SPEECH | HINTS AND TIPS | THE NEXT STEP

When you get to the end of the bar, your book is ready to go! You are an author! You now need to decide what to do with your book and what your next project should be. Perhaps it will be a sequel to your book, or maybe something completely different.

THE 'WRITE' LIFESTYLE

You may find information for your autobiography in family records and albums. You might also need to do research in the library or on the Internet.

To interview people and see places connected to your life, you may need only to walk into the next room or across the street. Sometimes, though, you may find yourself traveling much farther. Just like all writers, autobiographers need handy tools and a safe, comfortable place for their work. A computer can make writing quicker, but it is not essential.

What you need

These materials will help you organize your ideas and your findings:

- a small notebook that you carry everywhere
- paper for writing activities
- pencils or pens with different colored ink
- large sheets of paper for drawing a timeline
- index cards for recording facts
- files or folders to keep your fact-finding organized and safe
- dictionary, thesaurus, and encyclopedia

Find your writing place

Think about where you as a writer feel most comfortable and creative. Perhaps a spot in your bedroom works best for you. Possibly a corner in the public library is better. If your writing place is outside your home, store your writing materials in a take-along bag or backpack.

Create an autobiography-writing zone

- Play some of your favorite music or music your family used to play for you.
- Use earplugs if you write best when it is quiet.
- Decorate your space with family pictures or pictures of places or objects important to you.
- Place objects that hold good memories from your life around your space.

Follow the writer's golden rule

Once you have chosen your writing space, go there regularly and often. It is all right to do other kinds of writing there—such as a diary or letters—*as long as you keep on writing!*

CASE STUDY

Newbery Award-winning author Sid Fleischman writes at home in his old-fashioned house on the California coast. He enjoys the sounds of the nearby Pacific Ocean as he works at a large table covered with books and research as well as pens, pencils, and a computer.

Joanna Cole, author of *The Magic School Bus* series of books, spreads her notes and research materials across her bed. She reviews these materials in the evening, often with one of her four dogs sleeping on these papers. When Cole is ready to write, she sits at a desk and uses a computer.

GET THE WRITING HABIT

Before you can write a great autobiography, you have to build up your writing "muscles." Just as an athlete lifts weights or a musician practices scales, you must train regularly. You cannot wait until you are in the mood or feel inspired.

Tips and techniques
Set a regular amount of time and a schedule for your writing. It could be 10 minutes every morning before breakfast or one hour twice a week after supper. Then stick to your schedule.

Now it's your turn

Your personal heroes or villains

Heroes and villains are not just people whose faces appear in newspapers or on TV. Which people in your life do you admire, respect, or appreciate? Is there someone you know whose actions you dislike, resent, or fear? What has led you to feel this way? Have you ever been a hero or a villain?

Take 15 minutes to brainstorm ideas about your own personal heroes or villains. Describe the deeds or events that shaped your ideas about these people. Do you know why they act as they do? Are there ways that your villains are just regular people—acting in ordinary and even good ways? What has influenced your own heroic or villainous acts? When you have completed this activity, you will have a better idea of which characters will play important parts in your autobiography.

Now it's your turn

The best and worst days

Begin your writing practice with some timed brainstorming. Go to your writing place. Close your eyes for a minute and relax. Think about what the phrases "the best day" and "the worst day" bring to mind. Now open your eyes and write down these sentences:

- "The best day in my life was _____ because _____."

- "The worst day in my life was _____ because _____."

For the next 15 minutes, complete these sentences with any words that pop into your head. Scribble away! Let the ideas pour out onto the paper the way water gushes out of a faucet. Now stop. You are on your way to writing your own autobiography!

CASE STUDY

Sometimes autobiographers reveal family secrets that hurt or anger others. Adeline Yen Mah waited until her step-mother died before writing about her cruel deeds in *Chinese Cinderella: The True Story of an Unwanted Daughter.* Mah says this book still angered her brothers and sisters. Mah, however, is glad she wrote her autobiography, saying, "How can things change if no one speaks out?" She wrote the book for young readers. This autobiography is adapted from another, longer one Mah wrote for adult readers, titled *Falling Leaves: The True Story of an Unwanted Chinese Daughter.*

A LIVELY APPROACH

For hundreds of years, people wrote autobiographies to provide examples of proper behavior.

If these writers had acted badly or sinned, they confessed these deeds in their autobiographies. The authors told how they had learned to live better lives and paid for past evils. Many of these autobiographies involved faith and religion.

Other autobiographies were written by people who had unusual adventures or by famous military or political leaders, such as Benjamin Franklin (right). Ordinary people did not write their own life stories. This changed in the 19th century when ordinary people began to write and publish their autobiographies. Former slaves, Native Americans, and immigrants wrote about their experiences. Later more members of minority groups and women wrote autobiographies.

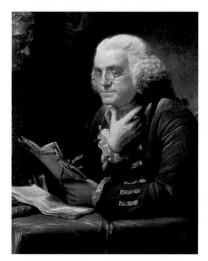

Today autobiography is a popular form of writing—one that people young and old, rich and poor use to understand and share their lives with others. Step lively and join this popular movement! Your life is important and worthwhile.

Now it's your turn

Your own family's stories

Stories are often passed down in families. Perhaps it is a tale of how parents or grandparents immigrated to this country. Perhaps it is the story of how the family survived a natural disaster, war, or other major event. Perhaps you often hear about how your parents met or the day you were born.

Brainstorm in your writing place. Think about which family stories are important to you. Which have you enjoyed hearing? Which have terrified or upset you? Which do you want to know more about?

Jot down the stories that stand out in your mind. You may want to ask family members for more information about these events, or you might research them in family records, at the library, or online. Perhaps you will ask family members why these stories are important to them. Your family's history and stories are an important part of your life story!

Tips and techniques
Decide what you will do about revealing any family secrets in your autobiography. What will family members say or feel if you reveal secrets? What will your responses be?

Now it's your turn

Your family identity

People's lives are shaped by many events, but particularly by their families. How has your family background been important in your life? Perhaps your family members are immigrants to this country. Perhaps your family's religion, race, or culture are very important to them or are different from most other people's. Possibly money has been an issue in your life. Is your family big or small? How has that affected you? Are you the oldest, middle, or youngest child, or the only child in your family?

Spend 10 minutes in your writing place brainstorming ideas about these topics. Then take 10 more minutes to fill in the blanks in these statements:

My family's _____ has been important to me because _____. When I think of my family's _____, I feel _____.

You have just found more strands to weave into your autobiography!

Tips and techniques
Don't be fooled! Some novelists use the word autobiography in their books' titles. The Autobiography of Miss Jane Pittman by Ernest G. Gaines is really a novel.

Tips and techniques
Autobiographies that focus on just one period in a person's life are often called memoirs. This French word means "memories."

FIND YOUR VOICE

Reading many books will help you discover your own style of writing—your writer's voice. Every good writer has a style of writing that is unique to that person. It takes practice to acquire this unique voice. Writers continue to develop their voices throughout their lives.

Finding your writer's voice

Once you start reading as a writer, you will notice how writers have their own rhythm, style, and range of language that stay the same throughout a book. Sid Fleischman has a playful voice that is very different from the serious ones of Gary Paulsen or Sally Hobart Alexander. Paulsen and Alexander write sentences with different rhythms from each other. Learning to recognize the different techniques writers use to craft their books is like learning to identify different kinds of music.

Writers' voices

Look at the kinds of words and sentences these writers use. Which writers provide many detailed descriptions? Who uses short sentences and sentence fragments? Who employs long sentences? Which writer uses an unusual comparison for humor? Think about which styles you enjoy reading.

> *It was so satisfying. Fighting the dread, the tension. Using athletic and intellectual abilities. Recognizing information from other senses. Taking the risk. Getting there. Every new venture increased my confidence. Every new trip fed my hunger for more, and farther, and faster. I was taking hold of my life again, and I felt alive.*
> Sally Hobart Alexander, *Taking Hold: My Journey Into Blindness*

When I woke up the next morning, there across the room was a ghost lying on a bed. He certainly looked like a ghost to me, with his bluish white skin, his hooked nose, his long, tangled white hair, and his white beard. His gaping mouth was wide open. This ghost had no teeth!
Joseph Medicine Crow with Herman J. Viola, *Counting Coup: Becoming a Crow Chief on the Reservation and Beyond*

But really I'm an improv artist most of all, and I don't even know what I've done once the moment is gone. A lot of times I look at footage of myself, and I'm like, Whoa! What was that? Rewind it. Rewind it. I have to stay with the step, right there, hold it in my head while it's fresh and make an effort to keep it there, or I'll forget all about it, it's gone.
Savion Glover (right) and Bruce Weber, *Savion! My Life in Tap*

I was dazzled. The moment he finished his act and ushered us gawkers back onto the sidewalk, I knew what I wanted to be. Someone else could be president of the United States.
I wanted to be a magician.
Sid Fleischman, *The Abracadabra Kid: A Writer's Life*

The problem was that I was alone. I had not learned then to love solitude—as I do now—and the feeling of loneliness was visceral, palpable. I would see something beautiful —the sun through the leaves, a deer moving through the dappled light, the explosion of a grouse flying up through the leaves—and I would turn to point it out to somebody, turn to say, "Look …" and there would be no one there.
Gary Paulsen, *My Life in Dog Years*

GET YOUR FACTS STRAIGHT

Your first step is to create a timeline for your autobiography. This will help you focus on which events, places, and other people to research further. Interview family members and check records such as birth certificates or photo albums for accurate dates, names, and places.

Tips and techniques
Use a tape recorder or take notes during an interview to preserve the information you hear. Not everyone is comfortable being recorded, so be certain to ask about this at the beginning of the interview.

CASE STUDY
Instead of dates or a timeline, writer Gary Paulsen (left) organized his autobiography according to the dogs that have been important to him. He titled this book *My Life in Dog Years* and devotes a chapter to each dog or kind of dog he has known.

Tips and techniques
Would an unusual way of marking time periods—such as Gary Paulsen's "dog years"—work well for your autobiography? Could your life be divided according to places your family has lived, jobs they have done, cars they have owned, or pets or hobbies you have had?

CASE STUDY

Some successful people—such as dancer Savion Glover and Chief Joseph Medicine Crow (right)—complete their autobiographies with the help of a skilled writer. That is why these works list two authors. Famous science writer Joanna Cole found it helpful to craft her autobiography with another writer. In *On the Bus with Joanna Cole: A Creative Autobiography*, Cole even explains how she worked with co-author Wendy Saul.

Now it's your turn

Matters of life and death

Draw a long line on a sheet of paper. On one side of this line, leaving some blank space at the beginning and end, mark off and label every year of your life. On the other side, mark and label the years linked to major events in your life: your parents' wedding, your brothers' or sisters' doings, starting school, attending camp, moving to a new home, or having a bad accident. Include important events for other relatives, too.

Now do some more research on this time period. Go back to the timeline and use a different color ink to add in important historical events that affected you or your family. These could include government elections, a local construction project, a war, or a natural disaster. Use the blank space at the beginning and end of the timeline for events that began before your birth or that are not finished yet. Refer back to this timeline as you research and plan your autobiography.

LIVE IN THE MOMENT

Help readers experience the world you know by describing it in sharp, bright, and clear detail. Draw upon as many senses as you can to re-create your world for readers.

Joseph Medicine Crow describes how, when he was 13 years old, he watched a re-enactment of the 1876 Battle of the Little Bighorn. His use of details re-creates the sights and sounds of this event:

What a spectacle! Hundreds of horseback riders were raising clouds of dust and filling the air with yells, war whoops, and gunshots. The black powder smoke from the guns added to the thick dust that covered the battlefield. I was excited and thrilled and then completely scared. I would take off as fast as my horse could run and then stop to look back. It all seemed so real!

Joseph Medicine Crow with Herman J. Viola, *Counting Coup: Becoming a Crow Chief on the Reservation and Beyond*

CASE STUDY

Astronaut Mae Jemison admits in her autobiography, *Find Where the Wind Goes: Moments From My Life*, "I am not sure that anything I recall before the age of two is more than a kind of 'thought insertion.'" Jemison, who is also a physician, draws upon family accounts and records to describe those early years of her life.

Gary Paulsen uses senses to help readers experience camping out in the Minnesota wilderness of his boyhood:

There was great beauty in running the rivers, especially in the fall when the leaves were turning. The maples were red gold and filtered the sunlight so that you could almost taste the richness of the light, and before long I added a surplus army blanket, rolled up over the pack, and I would spend the nights out as well. Gary Paulsen, *My Life in Dog Years*

Now it's your turn

Be sensational!
Look around your family's home. Or take your writer's notebook or laptop with you to your favorite outdoor spot to relax or play. Observe. Close your eyes and breathe deeply. Listen carefully. Run your hand over some rocks, along a tree trunk, or underneath a snowdrift. Now take 10 minutes to jot down all the details your senses revealed. Use these details to help readers experience your world.

GET THE PICTURE

Photographs, videos, or paintings of where you and your family have lived will inspire you as you re-create this setting for readers.

These resources are especially important if your family immigrated long ago or has moved several times. You may not be able to visit these former homes now, but your imagination can take you and your readers anywhere.

Adeline Yen Mah uses vivid detail to describe her first, lonely days as a first-grader in the Chinese city of Shanghai:

I turned a corner and now the sidewalks seethed with people and noise and commotion: coolies shouldering heavy loads on bamboo poles; hawkers selling toys, crickets in cages, fans, cold tea, candies, meat-filled buns, spring rolls, tea eggs and fermented bean curd; stalls and booths offering services such as haircuts, shaves, dental care, letter-writing, extraction of ear wax; beggars banging tin cups and chanting for a handout. Except for me, everyone was striding purposefully along, going somewhere.
Adeline Yen Mah, *Chinese Cinderella: The True Story of an Unwanted Daughter*

While Mah may have used just her own memories for this account from 1943, such details are also available through photographs and videos.

CASE STUDY

Artist Tom Feelings illustrated his autobiography, titled *Black Pilgrimage*. The African-American writer included colorful paintings he created while living in the African nation of Ghana. Feelings also drew many portraits of people in his own boyhood neighborhood in New York City and of black people in the southern United States.

Tips and techniques

If you are an artist, consider illustrating your autobiography with your own drawings, photographs, or paintings.

Now it's your turn

Live in the moment

Examine a photograph or painting of a place that was important in your family's life or your early years. Notice all the details, using a magnifying glass if necessary. Now write a 100-word description of that place as though you were right there. What do you see or smell? How hot or cold is it? What else do you feel as you brush up against objects or people in this setting? Who else is there? What do the expressions of their faces suggest that they are feeling? What noises or conversations do you hear?

Tips and techniques

Consider whether you will describe settings as you experienced them as a young child or as you experience them today. Perhaps you will do both.

CASE STUDY

Mae Jemison points out that settings look different to very young children than they do to teens or grownups. She lived in Decatur, Alabama, until she was 3½ years old. Jemison writes, "I remember hot, sunny streets and occasionally torrential rains. I had to look up at everything!" Decatur does not seem so huge to the astronaut nowadays.

DISCOVER YOUR HERO

You are the main character in your autobiography! In that sense, you are already the hero of your life story.

You may decide, however, that there are other heroes in your life—people or animals whose virtues you want to credit. It is your job as the author to help readers know and care about these major characters in your tale. To have this connection, they need to understand what these characters did and how their actions affected you. You must reveal what you thought and felt at different points in your life.

Build a picture

If your family has traditions that may not be familiar to readers, you should give readers background information to understand your characters' actions. Joseph Medicine Crow describes the four tasks—traditional acts of bravery and leadership called "counting coup"—that Crow men need to complete before they can become leaders or "chiefs" of their people. This information appears in his first chapter, titled "A Warrior Tradition." Similarly, Adeline Yen Mah describes the traditional relationships in Chinese families in a preface before she begins her autobiography. Savion Glover and Bruce Weber give a brief history of tap dance in the second chapter of Glover's autobiography.

> **Tips and techniques**
> *If your relatives will share personal letters with you, this correspondence may help you add color and fill in the gaps in your family's history.*

Now it's your turn

Life's historic moments

Look again at your timeline. Can you build a picture of the important historic events listed there? Quickly write a paragraph about one event. Now read it to see if it contains interesting details. Decide if you need to do more research about major events or trends that touched your own or your family's life.

Now it's your turn

Be proud!

Take 10 minutes to remember your success! Relax in your writing place. Think about what you are proud of having achieved. Perhaps you finished a project, helped someone else, or won a prize. Perhaps you are proud of working to overcome an obstacle in your life. What do you plan to be proud of next year? Five years from now? Twenty-five years from now? What are your goals for the future—and how are you already working to make these dreams come true?

On a sheet of paper, label three columns with "Past Achievements," "Present Achievements," and "Future Achievements." For five minutes fill in each column with as many items as come to mind. Take pride in having dreams and ambitions for the future.

Describe your hero

Use vivid details to describe your hero. One of the dogs whose companionship meant so much to Gary Paulsen was a stray he called Dirk. Paulsen writes that Dirk had "scraggly, scruffy hair and two eyes that glowed yellow."

Paulsen adds that Dirk's low growl was "not loud, more a rumble that seemed to come from the earth and so full of menace that it stopped me cold, my foot frozen in midair." This fierce behavior helps young Paulsen when Dirk defends him against neighborhood bullies. These bullies are just one of many problems Paulsen faced during a harsh childhood.

Tips and techniques

To describe yourself, tell what others saw looking at you at different periods in your life. Old family photos or videos may be useful, too. Describe your own appearance today using a mirror, photos, or videos.

YOUR HERO'S PROBLEMS

What problems have you overcome? Which problems are you still facing? When you permit readers to see the "real you," they will want to read more. Sometimes you may find that writing about your problems also helps you think of solutions to them.

Early in his autobiography, Joseph Medicine Crow— born in 1913—reveals the biggest problem he has faced:

[A]ll the boys of my age on the Crow Reservation were brought up in two ways at the same time. We were raised to be warriors but we were also expected to succeed in the white man's world. In a way, then, I have walked in two worlds my entire life.

Joseph Medicine Crow with Herman J. Viola, *Counting Coup: Becoming a Crow Chief on the Reservation and Beyond*

The power of names

Is there a story behind your name or the names of others in your autobiography? The mother of Savion Glover (left) named him "Savion" because she dreamed that he would be someone special— just as Christians believe Jesus is their savior. Glover's mother changed "savior" to "Savion" to avoid being disrespectful to Jesus.

Joseph Medicine Crow was called Winter Man as a boy. He explains how earning a new, adult name is part of becoming a grownup in Crow society, and he describes the exciting events that led to his new name. If you do not know how or why your name was chosen, ask family members. If there is a story behind your nickname, include that tale in your autobiography as well.

In the 1960s, Mae Jemison had to struggle against people's beliefs that a young, black woman could not succeed as a doctor or scientist. Later she fought some people's doubts that a woman would make a good astronaut.

Admit weaknesses

Readers have sympathy for heroes who admit their weaknesses. All human beings—and other creatures—have flaws. Recognizing and coming to terms with your weaknesses are also good first steps to overcoming them. Mae Jemison confesses that she "was a 'scaredy-cat' as a little girl." In particular, the dark frightened her. She recalls one time as a 6-year-old being tricked by other children to enter a dark basement. Jemison writes:

> *During the hour that my heart was stopped, I stood petrified on the stairs. My brain and the rest of my body continued to function. My mouth screamed. My eyes teared. I tried furiously to calculate whether it was possible to get to the bottom of the steps and turn on the light from the basement without the creature that lived in the coal bin reaching between the stairs and grabbing my leg.*
> Mae Jemison, *Find Where the Wind Goes: Moments From My Life*

Jemison explains that her desire to know has always been stronger than her fear. She writes that "my curiosity made me put trepidation aside and explore." In her autobiography, she frequently tells of her mother's strength and her father's support. Her parents—and some other relatives and neighbors —are also heroes in Jemison's autobiography.

CREATE YOUR VILLAIN

Have the problems in your life been caused by other people? Even though real people are not comic-book villains, sometimes people do hurt one another or commit evil acts.

Perhaps you or your family have experienced difficulties caused by situations beyond any one person's control—illness, war, or natural disaster. Identify the different sources of your problems and bring these to life for your reader.

What is the motive?

People commit evil deeds for different reasons. If there are human villains in your life, are they motivated by greed? By fear? By the desire for power? Or do they believe that their acts are not really evil at all?

Villainous acts

Adeline Yen Mah's greedy, selfish stepmother set cruel limits on her stepchildren. She gave them little food and told them:

> *The kitchen, garage, and servants' quarters are in the back. You are to enter and leave the house by the back door only. The front gate leading out of the garden is reserved for Father's guests. So is the living room. You are not to invite any of your friends home, or to visit them in their houses.*
> Adeline Yen Mah, *Chinese Cinderella: The True Story of an Unwanted Daughter*

Young Adeline also faced invading Japanese soldiers during World War II:

> *We children were supposed to show respect and bow whenever we ran past Japanese soldiers. Otherwise they would punish us or even kill us.*
> Adeline Yen Mah, *Chinese Cinderella: The True Story of an Unwanted Daughter*

Sally Hobart Alexander's former boss believes he is being kind when he discourages the newly blind woman from trying to teach again:

> *[M]y old principal shared a different philosophy. "Get married, Miss Hobart. Career goals don't always work out," he said. "Look at me. I wanted a career in the aircraft industry."*
> Sally Hobart Alexander, *Taking Hold: My Journey Into Blindness*

Gary Paulsen's parents drank so much that he left home:

> *For a time in my life I became a street kid. It would be nice to put it another way but what with the drinking at home and the difficulties it caused with my parents I couldn't live in the house.*
> Gary Paulsen, *My Life in Dog Years*

CASE STUDY

Fiction writer Sid Fleischman, author of *The Whipping Boy*, feels good about his life and career. He experienced some hardship and problems, but he does not blame other people for these difficulties. Fleischman writes in his autobiography, "I have had a life without villains. But it's been fun creating them."

Now it's your turn

Once a villain, always a villain?

When you were 5 or 6 years old, who or what were the "villains" in your life? Are they still the villains for you today? Why or why not? Who or what has changed since then? How has your understanding of people's motives changed in the years since you were in first grade? Take 10 minutes to ponder these questions and jot down your ideas.

DEVELOP YOUR SUPPORTING CAST

Add details or descriptions that bring minor characters in your autobiography to life. Just a sentence or two or even a few words can make an enormous difference.

A casual greeting and nickname communicate the close, teasing relationship between Sally Hobart Alexander and her brother:

> *"Hey, Sally-gally!" My brother, Bobby, on leave from the army, surprised me. "How's it going?" He held his arms out to me, and I flew into them.*
> Sally Hobart Alexander, *Taking Hold: My Journey Into Blindness*

Savion Glover helps readers see and hear the tap dancer who influenced Savion's career choice:

> *And I remember I followed Chaney into the dressing room, this big bear kind of a man with a low, rumbly voice, and he told me he had been a drummer before he was a dancer. And he was like, "You were doing some good rhythms on the drums," and I was just a little kid, so I didn't say anything. And he said, "You should try to dance."*
> Savion Glover and Bruce Weber, *Savion: My Life in Tap*

Now it's your turn

Be true to life

Jot down a few words of description or typical conversation for each of the people mentioned in your autobiography. Help readers to see or hear the people in your life.

Tips and techniques

An autobiography is not a diary or journal. People write diaries and keep journals to record for themselves what they experienced. They do not expect others to read these works. An autobiography is a narrative meant to be read by others.

Tips and techniques

Beware! Some novelists use the word diary or journal in the titles of their books. Sue Townsend's The Diary of Adrian Mole *is really a novel.*

CASE STUDY

Joanna Cole kept a diary when she was in junior high school. In one entry, she wrote about her science teacher. Cole reproduces this page in her autobiography to show how some of her girlhood ideas about people changed when she grew up. Her love of science, though, remained the same.

CHOOSE A POINT OF VIEW

You are obviously the best person to tell the story of your own life. But your viewpoint need not be the only one in your autobiography.

You may decide to include other points of view to tell at least some of the events. A different point of view may also be useful for giving background information. Before you write your autobiography, you must choose the point of view for it.

First-person viewpoint

Autobiographies are mostly written using the first-person viewpoint. The author uses the words "I" or "we" when describing himself or herself alone or with other people. The author lets readers hear what he or she thought, said, or heard at different times. The writer places quotation marks around spoken words or sentences. Sally Hobart Alexander uses first-person viewpoint as she tells about her difficulties learning to use a cane to guide herself:

> *As I ate breakfast the next morning, I prepared to swallow my pride. Drill Sergeant Zimmerman awaited me.*
> *"I could hear you banging up here all the way from the cafeteria," she snapped. "You're about as quiet as the drummer in a marching band."*
> *"Sorry," I murmured.*
> Sally Hobart Alexander, *Taking Hold: My Journey Into Blindness*

Alexander knows this teacher is critical, which is why she describes the sharp-tongued woman as a drill sergeant.

Third-person viewpoint

Some autobiographies also make use of the third-person viewpoint. The storyteller there follows the experiences, thoughts, and feelings of one character, but refers to this character by the person's name and "he" or "she." In *Savion: My Life in Tap,* chapters alternate between Glover's first-person accounts and Bruce Weber's third-person descriptions of Glover and his accomplishments. It is Weber who notes:

Savion is the first young tapper in a generation to have imitators, and almost all by himself he has reawakened an art form. It's a little hard to imagine such accomplishment in one so young. But in manner and appearance, he's still youthful —sweet-tempered, prone to goofiness, and with strangers as polite as a boy in church.
Savion Glover and Bruce Weber, *Savion: My Life in Tap*

Weber's viewpoint here lets readers view Glover through Weber's own perceptive eyes. This third-person viewpoint also gives background that explains Glover's achievement within the history of tap dance. In later chapters, Weber again uses the third-person viewpoint to provide more detailed information about the history of popular music and dance.

MULTIPLE FIRST-PERSON VIEWPOINT

The autobiography of figure skating champion Brian Boitano alternates Boitano's exciting first-person accounts with a third-person narrative about the history, rules, and techniques of figure skating.

Olympic medalist Boitano wrote *Boitano's Edge: Inside the Real World of Figure Skating* with Suzanne Harper. She wrote those third-person accounts. The authors here, however, decided to add several other first-person viewpoints to the autobiography. They include sidebars by Boitano's skating coach, other skaters, a professional skate sharpener, and the person who choreographs Boitano's skating routines. These multiple first-person accounts increase readers' understanding of Boitano. His coach, Linda Leaver, explains how special Boitano is:

Tips and techniques
Ask a coach, team or club member, or friend to write his or her own first-person account of your relationship. Add all or part of this narrative to your autobiography.

Brian was very coachable. If you asked him to do something, he'd be very open to trying it. He was also very truthful with himself and with me. If he was afraid to do something, he'd say so. That meant that I was always able to deal with the reality of the situation. Not every skater is like that. ... I never had to push Brian. Ninety percent of the time, he was pulling me.
Brian Boitano with Suzanne Harper, *Boitano's Edge: Inside the Real World of Figure Skating*

Truth versus memory

Sid Fleischman raises questions about truth and memory that all writers of autobiography face. He writes that he gave his 6-year-old sister a grass hula skirt for her birthday:

> *Given the trickeries of memory, I recall that she was embarrassed, hated the garment on sight, and refused to put it on. She recalls that she loved it and that she and her friends played with it for years. The other memories in these pages are absolutely true. I think.*
> Sid Fleischman, *The Abracadabra Kid: A Writer's Life*

You must think about how much of what you remember is true. You must also consider the possibility that you do not know all the truth about an event.

Omniscient viewpoint

Autobiographies usually are not told from the all-seeing and all-knowing—the omniscient—point of view. In fiction, this viewpoint lets the reader see and hear what all the characters do and think. In real life, people cannot tell what others are thinking, or see or hear faraway events. Sally Hobart Alexander could not read her sharp-tongued teacher's mind. Alexander did not learn that Mrs. Zimmerman really was a good-hearted person until they became friends months later. Adeline Yen Mah only found out about some of her step-mother's treachery after Mah's older brother overheard one cruel scheme.

Now it's your turn

Seeing other points of view

Choose one special event that you shared with family, friends, or classmates. Exchange written memories of this experience with someone who was there. Agree on the amount of time each of you will spend writing, when you will make this exchange, and when you will talk together about your first-person narratives. How alike or different are your accounts of this event? Would either of you want to include the other person's narrative as part of your own autobiography? Why or why not? Has reading the other person's account changed your own ideas of what happened at that time?

TELL YOUR STORY'S STORY

As your autobiography takes shape in your mind, it is a good idea to describe it in a paragraph or two. This is called a synopsis.

If someone asked, "What is this autobiography about?" these paragraphs would be the answer. An editor often wants to see a synopsis of an autobiography before considering it for publication.

Study back cover blurbs

Studying the information on the back cover of a book—called the blurb— will help you write an effective synopsis. A good blurb contains a brief summary of a book's content. It also gives the tone of the book—whether it is serious or funny. Most important of all, the blurb makes readers want to open the book and read it cover-to-cover! That is certainly true of this blurb:

> *When I was born, on October 27, 1913, there were no doctors or nurses around with their instruments, just a medicine woman who specialized in child delivery. With incense of burning cedar and the singing of sacred songs, I came into the world. I was singing, too, but they probably thought I was wailing.*
> Joseph Medicine Crow with Herman J. Viola, *Counting Coup: Becoming a Crow Chief on the Reservation and Beyond*

Make a story map

One way to plan an autobiography is to think of it the way filmmakers prepare a movie. They must know the main story episodes before the cameras start shooting. Before they start filming, filmmakers map out the plot (the sequence of events) in a series of sketches called storyboards. You can do this for your autobiography. The blurb and timeline you wrote will help you here.

Now it's your turn

Lights! Camera! Action!

Write a blurb for the autobiography you plan to write. Use it to identify the most important events on the timeline of your life. You are now ready to sketch the "scenes" for your autobiography's storyboards. Under each sketched scene, jot down brief notes about what you will mention about this event. Use this series of storyboards as a helpful outline as you write. If your book has chapters, each scene may be a separate chapter. Perhaps two or more scenes will fit together well in one chapter.

Write a chapter synopsis

Another way to plan your autobiography is to write a chapter synopsis. Look at the timeline of your life. Group major events there into six to eight categories, such as family history, first years, school, friends and family, hobbies and clubs, successes and setbacks, and future plans. Use each of these categories as a chapter. Following a chapter synopsis as an outline is one helpful way to stay on track as you write.

Tips and techniques

If you have a special hobby or interest, some important information about it may not fit smoothly into your autobiography's sequence of events. Put these nuggets of information into sidebars.

CASE STUDY

In Brian Boitano's autobiography, the authors frequently use sidebars to explain skating moves, rules of competition, and other tidbits from the world of figure skating.

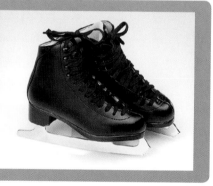

BAIT THE HOOK

Now that you have planned your autobiography, how will you catch and keep the reader's attention? You might choose a fascinating first sentence and captivating paragraphs to reel readers in to your work.

Your attention-grabbing sentence could be mysterious and suspenseful, hinting at something dramatic to come. That is how Sally Hobart Alexander begins her life story:

> *I walk barefoot on the beach, sliding my feet through the warm sand, not knowing that something is about to happen that will change my whole way of life forever.*
> Sally Hobart Alexander, *Taking Hold: My Journey Into Blindness*

This opening could be entertaining and surprising, if this style matches the rest of your autobiography. That is how the authors begin Savion Glover's autobiography, where they use bold type for great effect:

> *FUH-DUH-**BAP**!*
> *In a small dance studio on Manhattan's West Side, an argument rages.*
> ***Fuh-duh-duh-BAP!***
> *"Naw, naw!"*
> *The argument is wordless, but it isn't soundless. This is a dance troupe, Not Your Ordinary Tappers, arguing with their feet—conversations among shoes rattling on a wooden floor.*
> Savion Glover and Bruce Weber, *Savion: My Life in Tap*

Mae Jemison's opening sentence stirs readers' memories by echoing a question that many people hear during childhood:

> *"What do you want to be when you grow up?" Looking around the room I saw the magical board with the colorful felt sun, flowers, and trees that stuck without glue and I thought, "I know the answer to that." I waved my hand excitedly, arm straight up in the air. I could barely hold my response inside while the teacher called on the other five and six year olds. They said "fireman," "police officer," "mailman," "teacher," "mother." I had my answer. It was none of these. Finally the teacher called on me. Without hesitation, I answered emphatically, "I want to be a scientist."*
> Mae Jemison, *Find Where the Wind Goes: Moments From My Life*

CASE STUDY

In *Find Where the Wind Goes: Moments From My Life*, Mae Jemison compares events in her life to different kinds of wind. Each of her chapter titles extends this comparison. Some of these titles are "Whispers on the Wind," "Caught in the Eye of a Hurricane," and "There's a Change in the Air."

Sid Fleischman's opening sentences are casual and funny, matching the voice he uses throughout the rest of his autobiography:

> *I am astonished, when I pause to think about it, to discover myself to be an author of humorous novels for children. Or an author at all. I had a childhood much like everyone else's. What went wrong?*
> Sid Fleischman, *The Abracadabra Kid: A Writer's Life*

SYNOPSES AND PLOTS	WINNING WORDS	SCINTILLATING SPEECH	HINTS AND TIPS	THE NEXT STEP

HOOK YOUR READERS

You might decide to hook readers by beginning with a dramatic or exciting event. That is the choice that Savion Glover and Sally Hobart Alexander made.

Their openings plunge readers right into an important moment in the middle of a life. These autobiographies do not begin with the birth of their authors or even their childhoods. On the other hand, Mae Jemison begins very effectively with a telling moment from her childhood. At what point in your life will you begin your own autobiography? Your life story does not have to open with the first events listed on the time-line you created. The choice is yours!

Tips and techniques
Some autobiographies begin with a foreword by an expert in the author's area of success. Dancer Gregory Hines (above, left) wrote the foreword to Savion Glover's biography.

Olympic skating champion Peggy Fleming (left) wrote the foreword to Brian Boitano's life story.

Now it's your turn

Lively beginnings

In the library or a bookstore, look at the opening chapters of different autobiographies. See which techniques they use to hook readers. Which method do you enjoy reading? Brainstorm sentences and think of dramatic events you could use to begin your autobiography. Write out several openings to find the one you find most satisfying.

Tips and techniques

Many autobiographies begin with a separate dedication page—a few words, paragraphs, or even a full page in which authors thank people who have helped them in their lives or even in the writing of the autobiography.

CASE STUDY

Tom Feelings' dedication page in *Black Pilgrimage* is short but covers a great deal. He writes: "To my mother, Anna, whose constant faith and love kept me going; to all the Black people who encouraged me and helped me; to Africa—the reaffirmation of all my strongest beliefs in Black humanity."

BUILD THE SUSPENSE

After your exciting opening, do not let the excitement die. Keep and build suspense for your readers by crafting your autobiography in ways that emphasize the high and low points in your life.

Thrills and chills

Keep your readers on the edge of their seats by hinting about unusual, unexpected, or even unpleasant events that will occur in the future. This writing technique—called foreshadowing—will have readers eagerly turning pages to find out what happens next. Sally Hobart Alexander uses foreshadowing when she writes:

I think Brian was trying to break through to me and make me face the facts. But I was in sunny California with a handsome boyfriend, beaches, so much that was romantic. Nothing tragic had ever happened to me, and, like many young people, I believed that nothing tragic ever would.
Sally Hobart Alexander, *Taking Hold: My Journey Into Blindness*

The way Alexander phrases this statement makes us anticipate with dread the tragic events that seem sure to follow.

Now it's your turn

Life's struggles

Examine each of the storyboards or chapters you are using to organize your autobiography. For each one, make notes to indicate any conflicts you experienced during that event or time. Do not limit yourself to just one major problem. Maintain suspense by including these conflicts as you write your life story.

Character conflict

Do not ignore or try to hide your struggles or any setbacks. Sally Hobart Alexander lost some friends when she became blind, even though she also gained new friends. She often felt despair as well as determination. Savion Glover describes being nervous before performing onstage.

Which people or situations have posed problems for you? Have you ever gotten into arguments, fights, or other kinds of trouble? Be certain to include your conflicts as well as your successes in your autobiography.

Remember that people often experience more than one conflict at a time. While Joseph Medicine Crow bravely fought in World War II as a member of the U.S. Army, he also had to combat the prejudices of some American soldiers. When they called him "Chief," it was not often as a term of respect. He seemed foreign to them. Your autobiography may have several conflicts as subplots along with the main plot.

END WITH A BANG

Write an interesting ending to your autobiography. Make sure it leaves readers still thinking about you and the other people, creatures, or events in the life story you have told.

Tips and techniques
Some authors include a timeline of major events in their lives at the end of their autobiographies.

The climax

In fiction, stories build up suspense until they reach a climax. After this dramatic point, the characters' main problems are solved. People's lives often have such dramatic turning points, too.

For Savion Glover, the "pivotal show in his young career" came when he played a starring role as a famous jazz musician, Jelly Roll Morton (left), when the musician was young. You may have already experienced a dramatic turning point in your life. Perhaps such experiences are yet to come.

When stray dog Dirk rescued Gary Paulsen from boys who had bullied him for weeks, Paulsen felt enormous relief. He writes:

It was absolutely great. Maybe one of the great moments in my life. I had a bodyguard.
Gary Paulsen, *My Life in Dog Years*

CHAPTER 5: SYNOPSES AND PLOTS

Conclude your autobiography

A good ending often refers back to the beginning of your autobiography. This reminds readers of how much has or has not changed since the beginning of your book. Your conclusion may also contain your hopes or plans for the future. Sally Hobart Alexander looks to the future at her autobiography's conclusion. Her final words in this book are "Bring it on. … I'm ready to try anything." Savion Glover concludes his autobiography in this hopeful, determined way:

Tips and techniques
To create an autobiography that leaves readers feeling satisfied, avoid a bad ending. A bad ending fizzles out or ends abruptly because you have run out of ideas.

And if I have anything to do with it, tap is going to keep growing. It's going to have its proper place at last. I want tap to be like a baseball game, a football game, people coming to see us at Yankee Stadium. I want tap to be on TV. I want tap to be in the movies. I want tap to be massive. Worldwide.

Savion Glover and Bruce Weber, *Savion: My Life in Tap*

Now it's your turn

Choose your ending

Where will you end your autobiography? Will you end it soon after a climax that resolved a major problem in your life? Will you bring the autobiography right up to the present? There is no one right way to end an autobiography. Take some time in your writing place to experiment with at least two different conclusions to your life story to date. Put them aside for a while. When you reread them, see which one you like best.

| SYNOPSES AND PLOTS | WINNING WORDS | SCINTILLATING SPEECH | HINTS AND TIPS | THE NEXT STEP |

MAKE YOUR WORDS WORK

Words are the heart of your autobiography. They can pump life vigorously into this narrative. Choose words wisely to keep your life story in great shape.

A sense of life

Use as many of the five senses as possible to make descriptions come alive. Touch, sight, and sound help readers experience a late summer day along with 14-year-old Gary Paulsen and some farm dogs. Readers can hear that harvesting machine in the field and feel that collie's fur:

You could talk to them and they would listen. I'd tell them of my dreams, my problems, girls—endless talk of girls—as I sat there in the hot sun chewing on a straw, ruffling a dog's ears and watching the combine rumble around the golden field.
Gary Paulsen, *My Life in Dog Years*

Write to Excite

When you write action scenes, excite your readers with your word choice. Replace everyday words with bold, unusual ones. Have people strut instead of walk, and fly instead of jump.

Gary Paulsen uses vivid action words to describe his desperate reaction when he thinks a bear is about to attack:

> *I realized the gun wasn't loaded yet. I never loaded it while walking in the dark. I clawed at my pockets for shells, found one, broke open the gun and inserted a shell, slammed it shut and was going to aim again when something about the shape stopped me.*
> Gary Paulsen, *My Life in Dog Years*

A frightened Paulsen "clawed at" instead of "felt" and "slammed" instead of "closed."

Now it's your turn

Lively words

By yourself or with a friend, make a list of 10 everyday action words such as walk or fall. Then have fun brainstorming at least four unusual substitutes for each word. Perhaps someone would plunge instead of fall. Use a dictionary or thesaurus for extra help. Make every word count. Needless words are like extra pounds—they weigh your writing down when you want your autobiography fit and trim.

USE VIVID IMAGERY

Bring scenes to life by creating vivid word pictures with metaphors and similes.

Savion Glover uses a word picture to explain his physical connection to music and dance:

> *It's like my feet are the drums, and my shoes are the sticks. So if I'm hearing a bass sound in my head, where is that bass? Well, I have different tones. My left heel is stronger, for some reason, than my right; it's my bass drum. My right heel is like the floor tom-tom.*
> Savion Glover and Bruce Weber, *Savion: My Life in Tap*

These similes help readers understand the ways Glover's own body is like musical instruments he plays.

When Sally Hobart Alexander begins to lose sight in one eye, she uses a metaphor to describe what happens:

> *A pool of ink seemed to spill across the bottom of my left eye. I could only see through the top half. I tripped over a curb.*
> Sally Hobart Alexander, *Taking Hold: My Journey Into Blindness*

This does not mean that ink really filled Alexander's eye. This word picture explains that part of her vision went dark, just as ink spilling into a clear pool makes someone unable to see anything in that water.

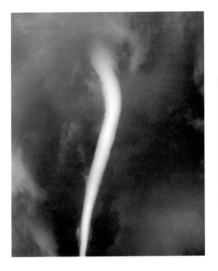

Tips and techniques

A metaphor describes something by calling it something else—for instance, a very active person is a "tornado." A simile describes something by comparing it to something else with the word "like" or "as." For example, a dewdrop sparkles like a diamond.

CASE STUDY

Sid Fleischman says that "imagery is a wonderful short hand. ... Figures of speech are hard to think up at first, but they get easier." Fleischman learned to love language while traveling around the United States as a young magician. He writes that his "sense of the color of language was awakened."

Now it's your turn

Imagine that!

By yourself or with a friend, make a list of 10 colors and textures. For each word, write down five similes. For instance, "As green (or red or brown) as a ..." or "As smooth (or sharp or rough) as the ..." How could you use these images or ones like them in your autobiography? Use a dictionary or thesaurus for extra help.

IN THEIR OWN WORDS

Using someone's own words is a great way to give readers a sense of that individual's mood and personality.

In your autobiography, you will re-create conversations and statements as accurately as you can. You may use tape-recorded interviews. Written materials —such as letters, diaries, or journals— may also provide you with words to quote.

Tips and techniques

In the dialogue you write, keep the slang and grammar mistakes that are sometimes part of everyday speech. Such lifelike dialogue helps readers hear the social class and regional background of the speakers.

Gary Paulsen is a boy rescued from bullies by a hungry stray dog. His conversation with this animal demonstrates Paulsen's generous nature and his loneliness:

> "That's it," I said, brushing my hands together, "The whole thing."
> A low growl.
> "You can rip my head off—there still isn't any more hamburger." I removed the Coke and handed him the bag, which he took, held on the ground with one foot and deftly ripped open with his teeth.
> "See? Nothing." I was up by this time and started to walk away.
> "Thanks for the help. ...."
> Gary Paulsen, *My Life in Dog Years*

Paulsen's speech shows readers how the strong bond between boy and animal begins.

Use dramatic dialogue

Conversations between people are a great story-telling device. They give information, create a mood, and add color. People may have talked quietly, argued bitterly, or comforted each other tenderly. Dialogue communicates and adds emotion to the events in any life story. It is a way to show rather than merely tell about an event.

Follow convention

Dialogue is usually written down according to certain rules. Each new speaker begins a new paragraph. You already know that what a person actually said is enclosed in quotation marks, followed or preceded by a tag such as "he said" or "she said." Sometimes, to give the sense of a real conversation, writers place these tags in the middle of a sentence. This placement adds another rhythm to the conversation, making it more lifelike. Memories, family photos, and videos will help you add descriptions of gestures, faces, and actions to dialogue.

Savion Glover's brother Abron speaks in an interview:

> "I remember I thought something crazy was going on," says Abron, who was three years old when his little brother rose up from a crawl. "He got up and walked on the knuckles of his toes. And not even walking. He was jumping up and down on them. Boing! Boing! Boing!"
> Savion Glover and Bruce Weber, *Savion: My Life in Tap*

Glover danced before he walked!

Tips and techniques

Use say, said, or wrote to introduce quotations. You can sometimes substitute words such as complained, whispered, or shouted for variety and when they suit the situation. Also vary how you introduce quotations and dialogue. Use tags in the middle or at the end of sentences.

USE DIFFERENT VOICES

Writing dialogue is a challenge even for experienced, skilled writers. Remember that the other characters should not sound like you. How characters speak often reveals a great deal about their background.

Here are examples of how people's speech differs in vocabulary, pronunciation, and rhythm.

A combination of cultures

A Crow man uses his imagination to overcome limited knowledge of English. He uses the Crow word for "baby" when he wants to buy eggs from a white clerk:

> *Then, he squatted over the blanket nest and cackled like a chicken. He then got up, pointed into the imaginary nest, and said "Papoose."*
> Joseph Medicine Crow with Herman J. Viola, *Counting Coup: Becoming a Crow Chief on the Reservation and Beyond*

Speech that communicates intense emotion

Adeline Yen Mah's stepmother lashes the girl with her words:

> *"Get out!" she snarled in a cold, distinctive voice. "I shall never forgive you! Never! Never! Never! You'd better watch out from now on. You will pay for your arrogance!"*
> Adeline Yen Mah, *Chinese Cinderella: The True Story of an Unwanted Daughter*

CASE STUDY

In her autobiography, Adeline Yen Mah sometimes uses the written version of the Chinese language—a method of writing called ideographs—as well as some Chinese words. These uses of Chinese remind readers of the place and traditions that shaped Mah's life.

Speech that is related to a particular profession

Savion Glover talks as a dancer:

> *I think in rhythms, and I talk that way too. It's weird, but I can
> say to you, "tickety BLOO kah tickety bloo kah SHUCK," and
> I'll know exactly what I'm talking about, and another dancer will
> too. I can have a whole conversation that way.*
> Savion Glover and Bruce Weber, *Savion: My Life in Tap*

Compressed dialogue

Sometimes dialogue works best without any introductory tags. Such
dialogue has a quick pace and rhythms of its own. Sid Fleischman
re-creates one conversation from his boyhood in this way:

> *"Ma! Did you throw out my magic?"*
> *She seemed pained and embarrassed. "Dad said*
> *you're too serious about this magic stuff. He said*
> *to get it out of the house and out of your system."*
> *"It's not hurting anyone!"*
> *"Dad says you'll starve."*
> *"Houdini didn't starve!"*
> *"Don't Houdini me."*
> Sid Fleischman, *The Abracadabra Kid:*
> *A Writer's Life*

Tips and techniques

Suggest that English is not a person's native language by including a foreign word or two in a greeting or excited remark. Use italics or a different typeface to identify these foreign words.

Readers can just hear that fast-paced argument.

Now it's your turn

Compress your dialogue

Try removing tags such as "he said" or "she shouted" from your dialogue. Does the pace of the conversation seem more natural? Does this pace better suit the mood and purpose of the scene? Can you still identify who is speaking? Some scenes work better with compressed dialogue that has no tags. If you cannot tell who is speaking without tags, you may want to work more to develop each person's voice.

BEAT WRITER'S BLOCK

Even famous writers sometimes get stuck for words or ideas. This is called writer's block.

If you have been following the writer's golden rule (writing regularly and often), you already have some ways to battle writer's block. Here are some of its causes and other weapons to use.

Your inner critic

Do not listen to that inner voice that might whisper negative ideas about your writing. All writers try out and then throw away some of their efforts. Sally Hobart Alexander first tried to write her life story as a work of fiction. She spent a year crafting that manuscript, but her editor rejected it. Alexander then spent another year working on the autobiography that became *Taking Hold: My Journey Into Blindness.* She tells people interested in writing, "If I can do it, you can, too."

No ideas

Have you run out of ideas? Read an autobiography by someone you admire or someone whose background or interests are similar to yours. See what techniques these authors used to write their life stories.

Now it's your turn

Step up and out

Don't sit still for writer's block. Take a break with a walk outdoors, a quick household chore, or an errand to the store. A short time away from writing may be all you need.

Find inspiration in fiction, such as a historical novel or mystery. Perhaps one has been set in a place or during a time that was important to you or your family.

Professional authors fight and win the battle against writers' block. Sid Fleischman believes that "the problem for the writer is not in finding ideas. They are as common as weeds. What to do with the idea that touches you and excites the imagination—that's the writer's problem." He adds, "Some writers are fast. Some of us are slow. Most of us are both. Each new book confronts the writer with story problems he or she may never have faced before. ... Today I regard a single page as a spectacular day's work."

> ### Tips and techniques
> Sid Fleischman suggests you end each day's work with a half-finished sentence. The next day, all you have to do to avoid writer's block is complete that sentence.

A writers' group

Writing may seem lonely. Some writers take heart by sharing their works-in-progress with other writers. They meet regularly in person or over the Internet with "writing buddies." These critique groups help fight writer's block by sharing ideas, experi-

ences, and even goals. Often members agree to bring a specific number of new pages to each meeting.

A change of pace

Defeat writer's block by changing your writing habits. If you normally brainstorm sitting still, try walking instead. If you usually like quiet while you write, add music to your autobiography-writing zone. If you write at the computer, try pen and paper. Vary your writing habits for each stage of the process.

CHAPTER 9: THE NEXT STEP

NOW WHAT?

Congratulations! Completing an autobiography is a wonderful achievement. You have learned a lot about writing and probably about yourself, too. You are now ready to take the next step in a lifetime filled with writing adventures.

A sequel?

Perhaps you will want to write a sequel to your current autobiography. Author Roald Dahl (left) followed his autobiography of his boyhood, titled *Boy: Tales of Childhood*, with an account of his adventures as a young man, *Going Solo*.

Sally Hobart Alexander followed *Taking Hold: My Journey Into Blindness* with *On My Own: The Journey Continues*. This book picks up where the first one ends.

CASE STUDY

Sid Fleischman recently combined his love of magic with writing in a new way. He completed a biography of one of the most famous modern magicians, *Escape: The Story of the Great Houdini*.

Write related fiction or nonfiction

Perhaps one of the events or people in your autobiography caught your imagination. You may be inspired to write in a new genre. Adeline Yen Mah recently wrote an adventure novel about a Chinese girl who fights the Japanese occupation of her country. In this book, titled *Chinese Cinderella and the Secret Dragon Society*, the hero also has to deal with a cruel stepmother. Sally Hobart Alexander has written books—told from the viewpoint of her children —about what it is like to have a blind mother. She has also written picture books based on her family's experiences.

Have you wondered what other people thought, felt, and acted like during events that were important in your life or your family's history? These thoughts might be just the inspiration you need to write a work of fiction. Perhaps you could expand a sidebar in your autobiography into a nonfiction book.

Now it's your turn

Make a story come alive

Brainstorm your story idea with pen and paper. List five historical events or settings from your autobiography on a piece of paper. For the next 10 minutes, let your ideas about people who might have been involved in each event or place flow onto the page. What problems did they face? How could they have solved them? Do not worry about complete sentences or punctuation. When you are done, you may have found the characters or plot for your story.

LEARN FROM THE AUTHORS

You can learn a great deal from the advice of successful writers. Almost all will tell you that hard work and occasional failure are part of the writing lifestyle. Yet even though few writers earn enough from their books to make a living, they value their ability to create and communicate through written words.

Joanna Cole

Joanna Cole (right) did not know any writers while she was growing up. She says, "I didn't know that a housepainter's daughter could become a writer." She held many different jobs before becoming a writer.

Today Cole is proud to be the published, award-winning author of many science books, including the popular *The Magic School Bus* series. Yet she says such success is "not truly what being a writer is about. Those are the rewards that come from outside me. The act of writing is why I write. There is nothing so wonderful as being in the middle of writing something, and it's moving along in a plodding, predictable way, when suddenly everything starts to go faster. The paper, the pencil, the computer—all of these seem to disappear, and I become lost in the process."

Sally Hobart Alexander

When she decided she wanted to write, Sally Hobart Alexander attended a writers' workshop to sharpen her skills. She tells young authors that there is no guarantee of publication for any author. She suggests, though, that kids read "endlessly. Read happily, then read critically. Read books for kids; read books for adults, even books for dogs, if such exist. Then, go out and live your life. Living doesn't mean sitting in front of the TV. Be a doer. Books come out of living, out of interacting with people and the world."

GETTING STARTED	SETTING THE SCENE	CHARACTERS	VIEWPOINT

CASE STUDY

Gary Paulsen answered questions from students during a visit to an Alaska school. In an online forum, an 11-year-old California girl who had just read *Hatchet* asked the author what advice he would give "to a kid who wants to be a writer." The author told her to "read all the time and write every day. Don't get discouraged."

CASE STUDY

Nevada author Julia Johnson writes about her childhood growing up on an Iowa farm during the Great Depression. She has turned her real-life experiences into fictionalized short stories published in several magazines. Her work, she says, "is intended to make the reader wish he too had spent his early years on an Iowa farm." Johnson writes whenever and wherever she can. "My first published story ("Auntie: Sage of Innocence," *Extension Magazine*) was written on my portable typewriter in a neighborhood park one summer while my high school daughter babysat."

PREPARE YOUR WORK

Let your autobiography rest in your desk or on a shelf for several weeks. Then, when you read it through, you will have fresh eyes to spot any flaws.

Edit your work

Reading your work aloud is one way to make the writing crisper. Now is the time to check spelling and punctuation. When the autobiography is as good as it can be, write it out again or type it up on the computer. This is your manuscript.

Think of a title

Great autobiography titles contain more than the author's name. Think of an intriguing, descriptive phrase to include in your life story's title. Figure skating champion Brian Boitano does this with *Boitano's Edge: Inside the Real World of Figure Skating.* This is a much more interesting title than *Brian Boitano: My Life as a Figure Skater.* Think about other autobiography titles you know and like.

Be professional

If you have a computer, you can type up your manuscript to give it a professional presentation. Manuscripts should always be printed on one side of white paper, with wide margins and double spacing. Pages should be numbered, and new chapters should start on a new page. You should also include your title as a header on the top of each page. At the front, you should have a title page with your name, address, telephone number, and e-mail address on it.

Make your own book

If your school has its own computer lab, why not use it to publish your autobi-ography? Using a computer allows you to choose your own font (print style) or justify the text (making margins even, like some professionally printed pages). When you have typed and saved the auto-biography to a file, you can edit it quickly with the spelling and grammar checker, or move sections around using the cut-and-paste tool, which saves a lot of rewriting. A graphics program will let you design and print a cover for the book, too.

Tips and techniques
Always make a copy of your autobiography before you give it to others to read. Otherwise, if they lose it, you may have lost all your valuable work.

Having the autobiography on a computer file also means you can print a copy whenever you need one or revise the whole autobiography if you want to.

REACH YOUR AUDIENCE

The next step is to find an audience for your autobiography. Family members or classmates may be receptive. Or you may want to share your work through a Web site, a literary magazine, or a publishing house.

Some places to publish your autobiography

There are several magazines and writing Web sites that accept memoirs from young authors. Some give writing advice and run regular competitions. Each site has its own rules about submitting work, so remember to read these carefully. Here are two more ideas:

- Send the opening chapter or concluding chapter to your school newspaper.
- Watch your local newspaper or magazines for writing competitions you could enter.

Finding a publisher

Study the market to find out which publishers publish autobiographies. Addresses of publishers and information about whether they accept submissions can be found in writers' handbooks in your local library. Remember that manuscripts that haven't been asked for or paid for by a publisher—called unsolicited manuscripts—are rarely published. Secure any submission with a staple or paper clip. Always enclose a short letter (explaining what you have sent) and a self-addressed, stamped envelope for the autobiography's return.

Writer's tip

Don't lose heart if an editor rejects your autobiography. See this as a chance to make your work better and try again. Remember, having your work published is a wonderful thing, but it is not the only thing. Being able to write an autobiography is an accomplishment that will bring you greater knowledge about yourself and your family. Talk about it with your brothers, sisters, or cousins. Read it to your grandfather. Find your audience.

Some final words

Writing an autobiography helps you understand yourself —why you think and feel as you do and what your goals and hopes are. You may find some of your ambitions changing. Your autobiography gives you more awareness of life's possibilities and problems. Completing this autobiography, though, finishes only the first chapters in your life story. With your new knowledge and confidence, you are ready to tackle many more real-life adventures. Someday you may write about those, too!

Read! Write!

And live your life with joy and reflection.

Glossary

chapter synopsis—an outline that describes briefly what happens in a chapter

edit—to remove all unnecessary words from your story, correct errors, and rewrite the text until the story is the best it can be

editor—the person at a publishing house who finds new books to publish and advises authors on how to improve their stories by telling them what needs to be added, cut, or rewritten

first-person viewpoint—a viewpoint that allows a single person to tell the story; readers feel as if that person is talking directly to them

foreshadowing—dropping hints of coming events or dangers that are essential to the outcome of the story

manuscript—a book or article typed or written by hand

metaphor—a figure of speech that paints a word picture; calling a man "a mouse" is a metaphor from which we learn in one word that the man is timid or weak, not that he is actually a mouse

motives—the reasons a person does something

narrative—the telling of a story

omniscient viewpoint—the viewpoint of an all-seeing narrator who can describe all the characters and tell readers how they are acting and feeling

plot—the sequence of events that drive a story forward; the problems that the hero must resolve

point of view—the eyes through which a story is told

preface—an introduction to a book

publishers—individuals or companies that pay for an author's manuscript to be printed as a book and that distribute and sell that book

sequel—a story that carries an existing one forward

simile—saying something is like something else; a word picture, such as "clouds like frayed lace"

synopsis—a short summary that describes what a story is about and introduces the main characters

third-person viewpoint—a viewpoint that describes the events of the story through one character's eyes

unsolicited manuscripts—manuscripts that are sent to publishers without being requested; these submissions usually end up in the "slush pile," where they may wait a long time to be read

writer's block—when writers think they can no longer write or have used up all their ideas

FURTHER INFORMATION

Further information

Visit your local libraries and make friends with the librarians. They can direct you to useful sources of information, including magazines that publish young people's work. You can learn your craft and read great stories at the same time.

Librarians will also know whether any published authors are scheduled to speak in your area. Many authors visit schools and offer writing workshops. Ask your teacher to invite an author to speak at your school.

On the Web

For more information on this topic, use FactHound.
1. Go to www.facthound.com
2. Type in this book ID: 0756535255
3. Click on the *Fetch It* button.
FactHound will find the best Web sites for you.

Read all the Write Your Own books

Write Your Own Adventure Story
Write Your Own Autobiography
Write Your Own Biography
Write Your Own Fairy Tale
Write Your Own Fantasy Story
Write Your Own Folktale
Write Your Own Historical Fiction Story
Write Your Own Legend
Write Your Own Mystery Story
Write Your Own Myth
Write Your Own Poetry
Write Your Own Realistic Fiction Story
Write Your Own Science Fiction Story
Write Your Own Tall Tale

Read more autobiographies

Ada, Alma Flor. *Under the Royal Palms: A Childhood in Cuba.* New York: Atheneum Books for Young Readers, 1998.
Aldrin, Buzz. *Reaching for the Moon.* New York: HarperCollins, 2005.
Bridges, Ruby. *Through My Eyes.* New York: Scholastic Press, 1999.
Douglass, Frederick. *Escape From Slavery: The Boyhood of Frederick Douglass in His Own Words.* New York: Knopf, 1994.
Esiason, Boomer. *A Boy Named Boomer.* New York: Scholastic, 1995.
Filipovic, Zlata. *Zlata's Diary: A Child's Life in Sarajevo.* New York: Penguin Books, 2006.
Goodall, Jane. *My Life With the Chimpanzees.* New York: Pocket Books, 1996.
Hawk, Tony, with Sean Mortimer. *Tony Hawk: Professional Skateboarder.* New York: Regan Books, 2002.
Jiang, Ji-li. *Red Scarf Girl: A Memoir of the Cultural Revolution.* New York: HarperCollins, 1997.
Kwan, Michelle. *Michelle Kwan, Heart of a Champion: An Autobiography.* New York: Scholastic, 1997.
Lewin, Ted. *I Was a Teenage Professional Wrestler.* New York: Orchard Books, 1993.
Lobel, Anita. *No Pretty Pictures: A Child of War.* New York: Greenwillow Books, 1998.
Mays, Osceola. *Osceola: Memories of a Sharecropper's Daughter.* New York: Hyperion Books for Children, 2000.
McPhail, David. *In Flight with David McPhail: A Creative Autobiography.* Portsmouth, N.H.: Heinemann, 1996.
O'Grady, Scott, with Michael French. *Basher Five-Two: The True Story of F-16 Fighter Pilot Captain Scott O'Grady.* New York: Doubleday, 1997.
Parks, Rosa, with Jim Haskins. *I Am Rosa Parks.* New York: Dial Books for Young Readers, 1997.
Polacco, Patricia. *Firetalking.* Katonah, N.Y.: R.C. Owen, 1994.
Rubin, Susan Goldman, with Ela Weissberger. *The Cat With the Yellow Star: Coming of Age in Terezin.* New York: Holiday House, 2006.
Sis, Peter. *The Wall: Growing Up Behind the Iron Curtain.* New York: Farrar, Straus, Giroux, 2007.
Spinelli, Jerry. *Knots in My Yo-Yo String: The Autobiography of a Kid.* New York: Knopf, 1998.
Stine, R.L. *It Came From Ohio: My Life as a Writer.* New York: Scholastic, 1997.
Tillage, Leon Walter. *Leon's Story.* New York: Farrar, Straus, Giroux, 1997.
Uchida, Yoshiko. *The Invisible Thread: An Autobiography.* New York: Beech Tree Paperback, 1995.
Yep, Laurence. *The Lost Garden.* New York: Beech Tree Books, 1996.

Books cited

Alexander, Sally Hobart. *Taking Hold: My Journey Into Blindness*. New York: MacMillan, 1994.

Boitano, Brian. *Boitano's Edge: Inside the Real World of Figure Skating*. New York: Simon & Schuster, 1997.

Cole, Joanna, with Wendy Saul. *On the Bus with Joanna Cole: A Creative Autobiography*. Portsmouth, N.H.: Heinemann, 1996.

Medicine Crow, Joseph, with Herman Viola. *Counting Coup: Becoming a Crow Chief on the Reservation and Beyond*. Washington, D.C.: National Geographic, 2006.

Feelings, Tom. *Black Pilgrimage*. New York: Lothrop, Lee & Shepard Co., 1972.

Fleischman, Sid. *The Abracadabra Kid: A Writer's Life*. New York: Greenwillow Books, 1996.

Glover, Savion, and Bruce Weber. *Savion! My Life in Tap*. New York: William Morrow and Co., 2000.

Jemison, Mae. *Find Where the Wind Goes: Moments from My Life*. New York: Scholastic, 2001.

Mah, Adeline Yen. *Chinese Cinderella: The True Story of an Unwanted Daughter*. New York: Delacorte Press, 1999.

Paulsen, Gary. *My Life in Dog Years*. New York: Delacorte Press, 1998.

Image credits

Index